O Virtue,

Where Art Thou?

A Study in the Book of Esther

Aaron Yom

SP

Seymour Press

O Virtue, Where Art Thou?
A Study in the Book of Esther

ISBN: 978-1-967034-12-3

LCCN:

SP

Seymour Press

Lanham, MD

Table of Contents

Biblical Abbreviations

NIV (New International Version)

NRSV (New Revised Standard Version)

NKJV (New King James Version)

Prologue

Esther is one of the finest stories in the Bible. It has stoked the interest of not only the doyen of the church but also newly born Christians. It is a wonderful way to introduce and re-introduce the key biblical themes to the believing community.

The story of Esther stands well on its own—it could be easily read and understood without any "commentary." However, as an experienced reader of the Bible, I see the need to add a few more attention grabbers to make the story come alive in today's setting. The story itself is great, but I want the world to see why it is a great story.

For this reason, I have added my "comments" and additional pointers that could help the readers engage more deeply with the book. My "comments" are never meant to exhaustively explain all the details or solve all controversies associated with Esther. For more detailed reading, I recommend academic works such as Anthony Tomasino's Esther: Evangelical Exegetical Commentary or Frederick Bush's Word Biblical Commentary on Esther. The main purpose of this book is to make the story of Esther more accessible and comfortable for the Christian lay person to read without marginalizing the intellectual flavor that comes with the story.

I kept the book in the story form so that the narrative structure is not altered too much, but despite its story format, it can be re-organized as a ministerial resource for sermons, biblical studies, or devotionals.

I hope the readers enjoy the story of Esther as much as I did, and that this little piece of extended form of the story can rekindle the passion to search for the deeper meaning behind the text of the Bible.

Author's Note

Reading the Book of Esther is never dull. It is actually "fun" to read this short story about a Jewish queen. It is like watching an action-packed movie. There is enough thrill and suspense for everybody to enjoy. It is truly one of the best entertainment stories from the Bible.

With a more prudent investigation, we can also see in and through the story the seesawing of sorrow and joy, defeat and victory, carnivals and lamentations, or humiliations and exaltations. These opposing categories create strong narrative waves that churn the emotions of its readers. With twists and turns, the story unveils the full spectrum of man's or woman's life journey.

The story of Esther is true to life, and at the same time, fairy-tale like, making it very difficult to tell the difference between the two. However, the detailed description of events points to the fact that it is more in line with the actual events of history than some literary fictions. Although this book is written like a theatrical script, it does not simply place meaning arbitrarily and subjectively just to please the ears of its audience.

It is realistic because its purpose is to "show and tell" the true picture of the human condition as well as the hope that shines in the midst of it. In the gloomy reality of the world, Esther injects a new vitality that stems from the glorious display of virtue. It helps us identify and live with virtue. We need this virtue because it is the key ingredient which sustains our own existence in the hope-bashing world.

I pray that, through the reading of Esther, every reader will find a new impetus to read the Bible and learn about what it reveals and why it is so important to us.

Chapter 1

King Xerxes and the Persian Empire

Esther opens with a simple statement. "This is what happened during the time of Xerxes"[i] (1:1). This helps the readers to adjust themselves to the historical setting of Esther. Although Esther does not provide a historical background of the story, having mentioned the name of the Persian king, we can safely locate the historical precedence of the story.

Xerxes was the son of King Darius. Darius was the fourth king of the Persian Empire, who ruled the land that stretched from West Asia to Balkans, including some parts of North Africa. By the time Xerxes inherited the kingdom, it became a colossal empire with its own culture and language that influenced many tribes and peoples around the world, as well as the empires to follow such as the

Greco-Roman Empire. Xerxes owned the Persian Empire from 486 BC to 465 BC. One of his well-known efforts was an attempt to invade the state cities of Greece around 480 BC, which turned out to be an utter failure on his part.

During the reign of King Xerxes, the Jewish people were living in exile. After a series of major invasions from surrounding nations, they lost their home country. There were two Jewish dispersions. The first dispersion occurred around 722 BC after the invasion of Assyrians that destroyed the northern kingdom of Judah and the second dispersion took place around 568 BC after the destruction of the southern kingdom of Israel. As a result, they were taken away to the foreign land. Only when King Cyrus ordered a decree for the Jews in exile to return home in 537 BC, some of the Jewish diaspora were able to come back to Israel. The return from exile and the restoration of the temple are recorded most extensively in Nehemiah, Ezra, and Haggai.

The story of Esther takes place during the reign of Xerxes, so Jews were already living throughout the land of Persia for more than 70 years. Since several generations had passed, they had settled down in all corners of the Persian empire, except for the few who decided to return to Jerusalem.

A Banquet in the Palace

If we look at verse 2, we can see that "in the third year of his reign he [Xerxes] gave a banquet for all his nobles and officials. The military leaders of Persia and Media, the princes, and the nobles of the provinces were present." The banquet lasted for "a full 180 days." Scholars often speculate that this was the time when Xerxes brought together his military and political allies to prepare for war against the city states of Greece, which is known to have taken place around 480 BC. That means that the banquet of 483 BC happened about three years prior to his march across the Sea of Helle into Greece.

Such a tremendous military campaign involving more than a half million soldiers most likely demanded a long-term planning. What better way to do this than to bring the allies and military leaders for a six-month long feast? It was a party like no other. Verse 8 reveals that "by the king's command each guest was allowed to drink with no restrictions, for the king instructed all the wine stewards to serve each man what he wished." There was a drinking binge and the sky was the limit. A king of such power and possession could only provide the best service, the best wine, the best food, and the best pleasure for the guests. They had fun like there was no tomorrow. This was the ultimate show of awe and wonder. If anyone can have a time of self-indulgence like the party in Susa with Xerxes, he has made it. He is at the top of the world. In this context begins the story of Esther.

The First Power Play

The drinking men seek to find new entertainment. What can heighten the spirit of these self-indulgent brutes? What else can the king do to show his majesty and glory to the world? What would help him top off the party with a bang? Is there anything missing for the party? Yes, the party is missing its hostess. So naturally, the king orders his queen to appear before the royal court of drunken men. However, for an unknown reason, Queen Vashti refuses to come (1:12).

Queen Vashti is perhaps the only "sane" person in the king's palace. She may be rejecting the war that Xerxes was planning and refuses to take any part in it. Or perhaps, she does not want to taint her beauty by going to a party of unruly, incorrigible, and foul- mouth drunken men. We can only speculate.[ii] Queen Vashti's gesture however spoils the king's party. In fact, all the men who are sitting at the king's table— only the most trusted servants and top-notch advisors sat at the king's table—are infuriated by the queen's disobedience.

In the world of power, disobedience is not allowed. Only complete loyalty and utter compliance to the order from the authority are permitted. There is no mercy. There is no second chance. The judgment is always final. Nothing evades the decree of the king. Besides, King Xerxes is known to be belligerent, aggressive, impatient, rude, and cruel.[iii] [iv] Who can blame him? Does he not have the power to do whatever he wishes? He has no quarrel with himself about killing people, ruining the lives of millions just to show his military might. He does not need to give an answer to anybody's complaint. Indeed, he is the epitome of tyranny.

Although he knew what he was going to do, nonetheless, to follow the royal-court protocol, he listens to his advisors. His advisors are not fools. They also knew what their king wanted to do with his queen. They exclaim, "Let it be written in the laws of Persia and Media, which cannot be repealed, that Vashti is never again to enter the presence of King Xerxes" (1:19). Queen Vashti is reprimanded severely. Vashti's mere no-show turns into an unpardonable sin.

The advisors' rationale for accusing Vashti of a great crime reveals a hidden agenda as they declare, "For the queen's conduct will become known to all the women." (1:17). To read between the lines, we see that they are not just talking about women's misbehavior. In actuality, they are afraid of losing power. Power is non-negotiable and non-sharable. It belonged only to this pagan despot, King Xerxes, and his loyal followers, who represents all men in the world. So, "man" symbolizes power whereas "woman" servility. The standing philosophy of the court is that power is the absolute commodity of the empire. No wonder there is no mercy in this court.

The Hypnosis of Power

Advisors' words are like a hypnotic spell of a serpent that enticed Eve in the Garden of Eden. How can anyone resist the sweet words of the wicked humming in the ears? Is there anyone who can resist the temptation of the evil one? Is there a righteous and merciful person in the court who can resist and say, "Be gone, you Devil!"? Apparently not. Power has suspended virtue. Xerxes the Tyrant issues a decree, and the king's edict is dispatched to all parts of the world, ordering that "all the women honor their husbands, from the least to the greatest" (1:20). The law has set up an inalterable Persian destiny. The male remains the dominant ruler of the house and the female the servient one. Power wins again.

Of course, power itself is not evil. It is what humans do with power that is problematic. Like a knife, we cannot blame the sharpness of a knife for our wrongdoings. In the hands of a surgeon, it saves lives, but in the hands of a criminal, it takes away life.

So does power. In the hands of God, it saves lives but in the hands of unruly man, it takes away life. What we need is a rein that can tame the power of the world. As we shall see, power can only be tamed by virtue.

The First Victim of the Powerplay

Because of the abuse of power, Queen Vashti is deposed. The subversive has been tamed. No rebel is left standing before the greatness of power. King Xerxes spares her life though. I do not think it is a consolation to the queen. Rather, it is more of a life- long humiliation inflicted upon her by the cruel king. Queen Vashti could only live in silence, tucked away in the history of the Persian Empire, nowhere to be seen anymore. She lives in obscurity, without any respect for her previous accomplishments. One single wrong move in the palace erases all honor and glory of the past.

An eagle has fallen. Her years in the royal palace, glory and majesty, beauty and charm, all have disappeared. The extraordinary returns to the trivial. Thus, only shame and grief remain with her. This is the reality of the palace. Behind the extravagance of the carnivalesque palace, there exists the tears of suffering and pain.

She joins the list of the thousands, if not millions, of victims who are depressed, oppressed, and abandoned, in the name of power. We can only hope that Queen Vashti of today does not remain in her devastation but rises above it. Listen to the first stanza of Maya Angelou's Still I Rise.

You may write me down in history

With your bitter, twisted lies,

You may trod me in the very dirt,

But still, like dust, I'll rise.

The relationship between King Xerxes and Queen Vashti in the first chapter of Esther reveals that, in the royal court of the Persian Empire, there is no mercy, no beauty, no temperance. There is only self- indulgence and the grotesque intoxication for more power. In short, there is no virtue. The Persian Empire has everything at the king's disposal, but virtue is nowhere to be found. So, the story of Esther continues and searches for that missing piece. A voice resonates in the thin air of the palace: "O Virtue, wherefore art thou?"

Chapter 2

The Emergence of Virtue

While the eagle had fallen from the pinnacle of her fame, descending to the valley of shame and destitution, virtue emerges onto the scene, rising from obscurity to its overdue majesty. Chapter 2 sets the stage for this emergence as it introduces two figures in the history of Jewish chronicles. They are Mordecai and Esther.

Mordecai and Esther, Strangers in the Land

Mordecai and Esther are a different kind of people. They do not belong to the palace. People in the palace enjoy high-fashion wardrobes, eat sumptuous food, and live a life of excess. By contrast, Mordecai and Esther who reside outside the palace have a humble outfit, barely eat three meals a day, and live a life of depravity. They are simple peasants. There is nothing fancy or grand about their status.

Also, they are not Persians. They are Jews. Jews are known for their exclusivity. The Jewish exclusivity is well-known from ancient times to the world of the 21st-century. Their exclusivity, though related to cultural particularization, stems from their religious cult. The feasts, food regulations, observance of Mosaic laws, marriage customs, sacrificial offerings, and hygiene regulations, all revolve around what God has commanded them to do, to be holy, to be separated as God's own inheritance (e.g., 1 Kings 8:53). They always hold onto a theologically and religiously unique identity.

For this reason, Jews are always proud of their national heritage, even though their nation had been completely demolished by Assyrians and Babylonians in the past. Their pride rests on the fact that they are chosen people regardless of their current social or political condition. For that, they are special. However, this sense of exclusivity, though it is their best merit, turns out to be their destructive vice.

Some Jews have become a stiff-necked people. This is the main criticism made by Stephen before his death. "You stiff-necked people! Your hearts and ears are still uncircumcised.

You are just like your ancestors: You always resist the Holy Spirit! Was there ever a prophet your ancestors did not persecute? They even killed those who predicted the coming of the Righteous One" (Acts 7:51-52). As the history of Jews shows, the danger always looms large. We can't be too stubborn or prideful of our own accomplishments, possessions, privileges, or heritage. We are all messy and messed up (Rom. 3:10). This is why we need to seek God's guidance, His ways of virtue, Holy Spirit's empowerment, and salvation that Jesus Christ has opened up for us all.

In Pursuit of Beauty

The palace is without a queen, so the king's advisors proposed to find a new queen. They recommend a beauty pageant. Who is going to be the presiding judge? Of course, it is King Xerxes. The qualification of a queen, which should be wisdom, honor, and glory, does not matter really. As long as the candidate wins the heart of the king, she will be the winner. What would please the king? Two qualities come to the fore: beauty and age. The decree basically reads: "Let the young woman who [can please] the king be queen instead of Vashti" (2:4).

This is the standard measurement of the palace. They look for the outer appearance of a young woman as the litmus test for someone to be the queen of the empire. By contrast, when seeking a right person for the job, God consistently goes after the "heart." For instance, when Samuel was sent to pick out the right person for the next king of Israel, God said to him, "Do not consider his appearance or his height." He adds, "People look at the outward appearance, but Yahweh looks at the heart" (1 Sam. 16:7). As a result, David, a young shepherd boy, was selected as king, though he had less of an impressive appearance compared to his older brothers. God was right, for David was "a man after God's own heart" (Acts 13:22).

This does not mean that the outer beauty needs to be set aside. As the medieval mystics often emphasized, the outer appearance and the inner quality must balance each other, for the two cannot stand without the other.[iv] For example, if we keep ourselves beautiful but have a wicked heart, the outer beauty is sucked into the terror of the dark soul. Nor if we invest our time and effort to keep an inner beauty but our outer appearance is untidy and unruly, then as the plant is choked by the thistles and thorns, the inner beauty will not be able to shine its light. Who has this balance of beauty?

Esther as the Next Queen of Persia

The second chapter of Esther turns to a lovely young woman named Esther. There is no hiding of her beauty, for it says, "[She] had a lovely figure and was beautiful" (2:7). In contrast to her unhidden beauty, Esther's Jewish identity is hidden. Her Hebrew name is "Hadassah," but as often the case is in those days with the Jewish diaspora, she does not go by her Hebrew name; rather she takes the name of "Esther", a Persian name. This name is given to her by Mordecai, her foster parent, to hide Esther's Jewish identity. Why would Mordecai want to hide Esther's Jewish nationality?

In those days (as well as in today's world), anti- Semitic prejudices are rampant all over the Persian Empire. Jews are consistently despised because of their inflexibility and exclusivism. It seems that Mordecai is smart enough to recognize this situation as he warns his foster daughter, Esther, to hide her nationality unless told otherwise (2:10).

Regardless, Esther is hand-picked by the royal officials and brought to the citadel of Susa because of her conspicuous beauty. In verse 8, we can see that Esther is taken to "the king's palace and entrusted to Hegai, who had charge of the harem."[v]

Hesed Virtue

In the following verse, it is noted that Esther "pleased him [Hegai] and won his favor." We can see from this that Esther is the embodiment of virtue. Virtue wins favor. Although the NIV translates the Hebrew word "hesed" as "favor," its main connotation is "kindness." For instance, this word is used to denote kindness of men especially extended to the lowly and needy (e.g., Prov. 20:28) or God's kindness, that is, His lovingkindness in condescending to the needs of His creatures (e.g., Ps. 144:2).

Virtue in this respect is strongly connected to the concept of "kindness." Without hesed (kindness), virtue cannot thrive. Thus, virtue is activated by kindness whereas kindness finds virtue. In the merciless and cruel world, virtue begins to sprout and takes shape, like a small plant taking root in the deserted wasteland. The beginning of virtue is not elaborate or luxurious. Rather, it has a humble origin. In the Persian Empire, it begins with a small personal transaction between Esther and Hegai, the king's eunuch. The sharing of kindness between Esther and Hegai is all that is needed to start the spark of virtue in this gloomy, unforgiving palace.

Esther respects Hegai like he is her father. In verse 2:9, Esther's virtuous behavior is denoted with two words that have similar meaning. The first word is "watitab" and the second word is "beanaw." The NIV renders this way. "She pleased (watitab) him and won his favor (beanaw)." We do not know why the Bible has these two similar words within a single sentence, but its main implication is the emphasis on Esther's good deeds and pleasant behaviors that attract the attention of Hegai. This shows that Esther is well-mannered and has been well-trained by Mordecai.

Mordecai's Guidance and Esther's Obedience

Mordecai seems to be the one who has trained her, for it is evident throughout the Book of Esther that Mordecai instructs Esther what to do, especially during a time when things matter the most (e.g., 4:7- 17). Mordecai, being a Jew, must have been well- versed in Hebrew Scripture, language, and culture of the time, which is his own source for the virtuous mentorship. We will come back to this point later, but it suffices us to note that Mordecai's intellectual and wise guidance has certainly contributed to Esther's success.

Notwithstanding Mordecai's fine mentorship, we have to give credit to Esther. Had Esther refused to obey and rather rebelled against her father's instructions, behaving like an unruly teenager, she would not have made it to the top.

Esther keeps her virtue. Her virtue is wise obedience. She obeys those who are giving her good advice. She listens attentively and intelligibly and acts according to the best manner that she knows how.

She chooses to do good. When we do the right things, it pleases others. So, Esther's hesed (kindness) never comes about out of twisted motivations. Esther's hesed is the result of her well-nurtured and well-mannered nature. Her hesed certainly is noticeable, for "Esther won the favor of everyone who saw her" (2:15b). The word "favor" here in Hebrew is "hen," which is comparable to the word hesed. Esther's hesed (kindness) is indeed winning hen (favor), and this is the result of virtue connecting the dots between good things that Esther is doing and the favor that people are willing to show because of it.

The Strength of Virtue

However, Esther's virtue seems too feminine. It does not align well with the hard reality of the world. Is not the world armed with teeth and claw, ready to tear down whoever or whatever is not fit to be in the world? As evolutionists would affirm, the world is not made for the weak. Only the strong or the fittest survive. The weak are only there as the prey for the strong. Innocence and charm do not matter much to the harsh dynamics of nature. The brute force of nature sweeps away the debris and trinkets, leaving behind only the strongest rock that is sturdy enough to resist the storm.

But, by contrast, the Bible emphasizes the power of virtue that wells up from what is weak and innocent. From a biblical perspective, the weak carries its own strength, for God works even more powerfully when we are weak (2 Cor. 12:9).

So, virtue is powerful after all. Its power has often been underestimated due to its association with the feminine qualities. As we shall see over the course of Esther's life, the power of virtue is more dynamic and influential than what it is taken for. But for now, we return to the theme of "favor."

The Light of Virtue

Virtue attracts the attention of the world. Its beauty and charm are irresistible. As the female birds are attracted to the beauty of the male birds and their showmanship, it is natural for people to be inspired by and enthralled with the beauty of virtue. Even the fiercest of men, Xerxes, takes notice of Esther's beauty.

Verse 2:17a confirms and says that "the king was attracted to Esther more than to any of the other women, and she won his favor (hesed) and approval more than any of the other virgins." The word "hesed" appears again. Esther's hesed wins her crown as "he [Xerxes] set a royal crown on her head and made her queen instead of Vashti" (2:17b). This is a great time of celebration for the palace as well as the entire kingdom. Finally, the world has recovered the lost virtue. At last, a light of hope shines in this deplorable, hideous, obnoxious house of power-thirsty mongrels.

John must have felt the same way when he realized that Jesus Christ was the light of the world. However, as it is noted in John 1:5, the "light shines in darkness and the darkness has not understood it." The light represents Jesus Christ and the darkness the blindness of this world. The light of Christ is the missing virtue that the world needs, but as John laments, due to worldly blindness, no one recognizes it for all are blinded by their own vices.

Nonetheless, whether we recognize it or not, the light has come and broken through the darkness. Just like the creation scene, God's word has broken through the world of darkness, and like the symphony of Joseph Haydn's "The Creation," both the powerful bang and the soft harmony of strings reverberate throughout the world, awakening the deaf and the blind to see the light of virtue that now shines to every corner of the world. Indeed, such an occasion deserves a celebration (2:18), though people may not know really what they are celebrating.

An Advocate of Virtue

Before we end, we need to briefly talk about a short addition to Esther's ascend to her queenship. In verse 2:20, the focus of the story shifts to Mordecai. Mordecai is described as Esther's foster parent (2:15). According to the brief description, it seems that Mordecai is actually Esther's cousin since Esther is the daughter of Mordecai's uncle. Due to the lack of detailed background information, we can only speculate here. More than likely, Esther became an orphan, for Mordecai had to take her into his household as an adopted child.

This is another key aspect of virtue. Virtue needs an advocate. Our advocate embraces us when we are alone, vulnerable, depressed, and oppressed. It is like a good father who makes us laugh when we are sad, who speaks the words of hope when we are going through hopeless situations, who rekindles our passion to pick ourselves up when we are down, and who takes our hands even when we are rejected. Our advocate's constant guidance and nurturing is needed for virtue to transform our inadequacies to divinely inspired hen (favor), ensuring that it will not fall to the ground and disappear without a trace like Queen Vashti.

Who is our true advocate? Jesus brought up this issue for his disciples before his death on the cross. Jesus told his disciples that he was going to leave them, but he ensured them that there will be a second comforter, the Advocate, who will come and be with them (Jn. 14:16). This Advocate is none other than the Holy Spirit. This is why it is so important for us to be filled with the Holy Spirit. I could list many other reasons for us to be empowered by the Holy Spirit, but I must emphasize here that the most important aspect of spiritual empowerment is bearing the fruit of the Spirit (Gal. 5:22-23): love, joy, peace, forbearance, kindness, goodness, faithfulness, gentleness and self-control. This represents the core of what virtue is all about. Virtue has nine branches and each of these nine branches bears the fruit of the Holy Spirit. Without the Holy Spirit, virtue cannot be sustainable.

Mordecai's Heroism

Going back to Mordecai, we read in verse 2:21 that he has detected a plot to kill the king of Persia. Apparently, two of king's officials had a grudge against King Xerxes and they conspired to assassinate him. Mordecai, with his watchful eyes and open ears, detects this wrongdoing and reports to Queen Esther, and she in turn, reports to the king. The two conspirators are finally captured and killed. We can see a glimpse of Mordecai's character.

He is alert and watchful. He does not permit a single mishap to slip pass him. More importantly, when he sees wickedness slowly crouching to attack the innocent, he does not stand idle, but takes the matter into his own hands, even putting his life on the line. He does not cower even before the assassins. Who are assassins? They are ruthless, merciless, and lawless men, who have drawn their sword to commit the greatest atrocity in the history of the Persian Empire. If anyone gets in their way, surely, he will be cut down in the blink of an eye. Nonetheless, Mordecai's courage moves him to take down the evil with his own bare hands.

Queen Esther is loyal to Mordecai and allows him to take the credit for the heroic effort of capturing the assassins (2:22). As with all other events that happened to the king, this particular incident is recorded in the book of the annals of the king (2:23). However, King Xerxes forgets about

Mordecai's deed and skips the reward ceremony. Mordecai's heroism is forgotten.

The work of righteousness may not always be rewarded, let alone, recognized by the public. In fact, the doers of righteousness are often persecuted. We know too well what happened to the Old Testament prophets. They declared God's words of righteousness to correct the people's wrongdoing, but they were ridiculed, shamed, beaten, imprisoned, and killed. Just because they stood up for their faith, they were put to death by stoning, being sawed in two, and killed by the sword (e.g., Heb 11:37).

The same type of treatment is given to Jesus, the Righteous One. He did nothing but righteous deeds, dining with sinners, healing the sick, accepting to his circle the socially ostracized, giving hope and future to the hopeless, and bringing the kingdom of God to the lost people. For that, he was cursed, beaten, spit at, and crucified on the cross. The death of the Righteous One is the climactic point of the world gone mad. It does not know how to treat the Righteous One. It has forgotten about the righteousness of God. I just hope that the voice of the one calling in the wilderness continues to make some noise and wake up all of us from our dogmatic slumber. Let us give our ears and heed to the voice that says, "Repent, for the kingdom of God is at hand."

Chapter 3

Haman's Scheme

In this chapter, the story turns again to the hard reality of the power struggle that goes on in the palace. It centers around a new political figure, Haman. Haman is up there at the highest echelon. His power ranks only second to King Xerxes. Because of his powerful status, he enjoys people stooping down to him. Even "all the royal officials at the king's gate bowed down and paid honor to Haman" (3:2). Sociologist Joe Magee once said that it is less likely for those who are power driven to take the perspective of others into account. In other words, the powerful people tend to be selfish. They want to enjoy the power that they have and all the added perks that come with it such as the ability to control people.

Haman's Dangerous Power Display

Psychologist Dick Pels may be right when he said, "If we need great men for their greatness, we must hence always guard against their darkness." As we shall see, in Haman's case, Pels' warning is all the more applicable. Haman's selfish ambition almost wiped out the entire Jewish population.

His ascension to the top-ranking position may not have been easy. He probably had to compete with his foes, or even his friends, often killing them, to come to where he is. The power struggle that takes place in the palace is merciless. This is evident in the way that Absalom tried to overtake his father's throne. David had to flee from his palace, giving up the throne (temporarily) to his rebellious son. He was betrayed by his own son and he had to run for his life while "the whole countryside wept aloud" for him (2 Sam 15: 23). Indeed, the betrayal and deceptions are common in the struggle for power. Whatever it takes, the greed for more power drives men to do things that defy any moral standard that we have in this world.

Haman's life is going smoothly. There is no hindrance. He enjoys his life of power because there is no one in the entire kingdom that can oppose or disrespect his hard-earned power. But, one day, an individual without a distinguished rank or background stands up to him. He is Mordecai. He refuses to bow down to Haman (3:2b). The royal officials ask him for many days, "Why do you disobey the king's command?" Mordecai keeps his mouth shut and refuses to bow down to Haman. Mordecai's attitude is clearly confrontational and provocative.

Mordecai's Resistance

The Book of Esther is silent on why Mordecai is behaving this way. In Targum Sheni, an Aramaic translation and elaboration of the Book of Esther, the reason is specified, one religious and another cultural.

It is religious since Jews can only bow to God. It is cultural since Jews did not bow to their enemies, like the descendants of Amalekites. Haman is an Agagite. He is Agag redivivus, the king of the Amalekites, the enduring enemy of Jews. As contended by scholars like Andre LaCocque, the bottom-line reason for Mordecai's rebellion is that he is a Jew. His Jewish heritage prevents him from bowing to Haman. How can Mordecai bow down to the enemy of the Jews and God?

Mordecai's refusal to stoop before Haman incites a new power struggle. As it is customary for Haman, knowing that only the winner remains standing in the power struggle, he searches for a way to quench the rebellious attitude of Mordecai. He plots an elaborate scheme to "destroy all Mordecai's people, the Jews, throughout the whole kingdom of Xerxes" (3:6). It is an unabashed expression of his new-found purpose—to destroy all Jews living in Persia.

The Rebirth of Amalekites' Atrocity Against the Israelites

Haman is re-enacting the atrocity committed by Amalekites against the Israelites at Rephidim. They attacked the wandering Israelites from the rear of the long line of procession on their way to the promised land of Canaan, killing mostly the women and the children (Deut 25:18). Such a brutal act is not only immoral but also abominable. It defiles the attackers, revealing that there is nothing in them that is good (Ps. 14:1).

"How much less man, who is abominable and filthy, who drinks iniquity like water" (Job 15:16)! Just because one person refuses to bow down, could an individual be so cruel to kill him and his family as well as the entire Jewish population? If we have power as great as what Haman had, this is not at all impossible. Who can stop him? If Haman can come up with a reasonable explanation to the king, the only one who is above him, he is home free. He can make it happen. If he can make it happen, who can stop him?

Haman's Irresistible Proposal

So, Haman, as always, with his eloquent speech and pleasing gestures, speaks to King Xerxes. He knows how to play the game. Like a savvy businessman, Haman begins to pitch his sales. He comes up with a proposal that the king would not reject. His proposal consists of the following. First, he identifies the problem that Xerxes may dread the most—i.e., Xerxes perfect kingdom being tainted by a group of rebels. Haman tells that the Jews are rebellious because they do not obey the king's law (3:8). This is a big problem for Xerxes, or for any kingdom. Rebellion must not be tolerated. Only the complete loyalty to the king's decree and laws are honored. The Roman Empire made this principle into a science. It became a well-known standard as Pax Romana (Latin for "Roman Peace"). Anyone or any people who stirs up trouble against the empire had to be cut down mercilessly. In the name of peace, thousands of lives had to be sacrificed for the sustenance of the Roman Caesars.

A similar idea is running through the mouth of Haman. He knew that Xerxes does not tolerate rebels. So, he pivots on this point and urges the king to deal with the rebellious Jews immediately. Otherwise, his kingdom may suffer. The thorn in the flesh must be pulled out and Haman is willing to do that for Xerxes. Xerxes has no reason to say "no." If the thorn can be removed and Haman, the second in command, is willing to do it for him, why would he say "no" to the proposal?

Moreover, Haman suggests one more thing. He says to the king, "I will give ten thousand talents of silver to the king's administrators for the royal treasury" (3:9). The weight of silver may have been 340 tons. It is very difficult to calculate the value of this weight, but it could run up to $300 million dollars in today's money. Essentially, Haman is bribing Xerxes. Haman seems to have an insatiable appetite for the king's favor. Rather than gaining the royal favor through virtuous acts, Haman is trying to "buy" the king's favor with his offer of money. This is the greatest travesty against justice, for "a bribe blinds the clear-sighted and subverts the cause of the just" (Exodus 23:8).

A Misguided Favor

Xerxes has no reason to refuse Haman's offer. By getting rid of the Jews, Xerxes will not only restore peace throughout his kingdom but also be millions of dollars richer. Who can resist this offer? However, Xerxes, who is already rich, refuses to stoop down to the level of Haman's craftiness. He orders Haman, "Keep the money and do with the people as you please" (3:11). Xerxes supports Haman, because after all, he is his viceroy, a loyal servant to the king. He must support him, for Haman is trying hard to preserve the kingdom.

Haman gains the king's favor. But the favor he earned is not natural. The favor that Haman has earned is the result of a business deal, or more precisely, a power deal. The balance of power must be maintained in the palace. Xerxes may need to keep Haman as his viceroy who can do the dirty work for him, fending off any attack that comes his way. Finally, the king's edict has been drawn and sent to the king's empire (3:12). His words are infallible and irrevocable. As LaCocque notes, "royal decree is frozen and monoglossic" because the king's words are the embodiment of the royal establishment.

The order is simple: "destroy, kill and annihilate all the Jews—young and old, women and children" (3:13). Like the king's previous edict concerning "women," which reduced them to a social aberration that needs to be tamed by "men," now the edict is directed to the Jews who are considered a social nuisance that needs to be eradicated for the good of the nation. At this moment, the Jews have the same fate as the sacrificial lamb that is sent to the slaughter (Isa. 53:7).

While the king and Haman are drinking the finest wine in the land (3:15), the whole country is in uproar. Thousands, if not, millions of innocent blood may be shed, because of these two ruthless men's business deal. Fate lies in the "pur" (lot) thrown by Haman. Though not specified in the Bible, the Jewish diaspora once again cries to God for help. Every house and every corner where there are Jews, there is weeping and sobbing (4:3). They all know that the king's edict is final. There is no one who is stronger or more powerful to revoke the king's order. It is hopeless. The angel of death that covered the night during the exile from Egypt is now hanging over the Jews living in Diaspora. Who can save them? The drama continues in the absence of virtue.

Chapter 4

The Call of Virtue

We see in this chapter Mordecai bursting onto the scene tearing his clothes in utter desperation. He puts on sackcloth and ashes as with all Jews in the kingdom. This is done when the Jewish people grieve for the death of their loved ones. It is much more significant than wearing a dark suit for the funeral in our days. Sackcloth and ashes symbolize utter humility, debasement, grief, and sorrow. All these negative sentiments are jammed packed in the wearing of sackcloth and ashes. In such a hopeless situation, they may as well wear them, even though no one has died yet. The king's edict cannot be revoked and there is no hope for them. Who can fight against the mighty king of Persia? Certainly not the group of ragtag Jews. They can do nothing except face their immanent doom by weeping and wailing.

The Dirge of Jewish Diaspora

Due to their turbulent history, Jews often sang dreadful dirge that triggers sad tears in our eyes. The tunes easily push our psychological button, and often, our emotion runs wild, recalling the pain and sorrow that we went through in our difficult years. Jews are one of the most persecuted people on this planet. Their life is full of misery, if not, "close calls." They are hated, mocked, ostracized, rejected, and often killed just because of their Jewish identity. Throughout the world, a deep-seated anti-Semitism has been created due to religious and cultural differences.

As many Jews lament in sackcloth and ashes, Mordecai breaks the news to Esther. He sends a message to Esther through the king's eunuch and orders her "to go into the king's presence to beg for mercy and plead with him for her people" (4:8).

Mordecai does not simply ask her to go to the king but forcibly "orders" her to go to the king. It shows the urgency of the situation.

Mordecai's Admonition

Esther sends a message back to Mordecai (4:10). She tells him that it is not possible for her to go to the king unless the king summons her first. If she breaks this law, she will be put to death. However, there is one exception. Her life may be spared if the king extends his scepter and dismisses her unwarranted intrusion. This is a royal protocol. It applies to not only the Persian Empire but also the kingdom of God.

No one can come to God. We all fall short of His glory (Rom 3:23). Without God reaching out to us, there is no way for us to come before God. This is why God's election is a key theological theme of the Bible. As Paul notes, we can come to God because "in love he predestined us for adoption as sons through Jesus Christ, according to the purpose of his will" (Eph 1:4-5). We can be with God only because God has chosen us before the foundation of the world.

Despite the similarities between the worldly kingdom and God's kingdom, they are utterly different. Xerxes' summon is always for his own sake. It is not for the sake of the one who is summoned. However, God's election is for the sake of the one who He is calling. He calls us so that we can have eternal life (Jn. 3:16). What an amazing grace this is! We who are not worthy to be in the presence of the King of Kings are now freely invited to stand in His presence forever.

But how can we sinners stand before the Holiest of the Holy? Like the royal protocol, our sins are forgiven as our Lord and Savior extends His scepter of mercy to us. In this respect, the king's scepter represents the cross of Jesus Christ. God's scepter has been extended in and through the cross. Indeed, the cross represents the forgiveness of our sins through the death of the Son of God. There is no more shame. There is no more dishonor. There is no more death. Thanks to Christ and His sacrifice, only the glory of new creation (2 Cor 5:17) remains with us as we are called His children. With this new identity, we are now made righteous and able to stand tall before the throne of God.

Esther's Dilemma

Esther tells Mordecai that no one is to approach the king without his invitation (4:11). The Queen is not an exception. She must abide by the rules set forth by the royal court or face the consequences. Since the regulations in the palace are very strict, Esther knows that there is no "flexibility" and that she may die if she were to flex the rules. Her intention is transparent. She does not want to go to the king and risk her life. Potentially, she can lose everything, even her life.

Virtue is slipping away. Virtue has been overwhelmed by fear. Esther's ego kicks in and she wants to protect her life.

She sees herself first. "Me- first" is an Achille's heel for virtue. It chokes virtue and diminishes its vitality. It is stated (2:20) that, while Esther was under Mordecai's care, when she was young, she followed his instruction to a tee. There was no hint of disobedience. But not this time.

Mordecai is not happy hearing the news from Esther (4:12). Mordecai's words thunder like a great tempest. He takes an extreme measure and warns Esther that her life is not going to be spared when all Jews perish. He points out that her life is never guaranteed because she is also a Jew. No secret is eternal. Even if she may survive this holocaust, her life will never be guaranteed. Once Xerxes finds out who she really is, she will certainly meet the same fate as any other Jew. It seems like a threat, but it is more like a fact. The king's palace is full of life-threatening hazards that one wrong move can lead to a devastating consequence like Queen Vashti.

Mordecai is not done. He gives Esther another reason for her to act as soon as possible. If she does not act now, someone else will in her stead, and having faith in God, Mordecai emphasizes the possibility that "deliverance for the Jews will rise from another place" (4:14). As the saying goes, if we do not praise the Lord, we will lose our chance, and in our place, even "the stones will cry out" (Luke 19:40).

Although the word "God" is not mentioned here, it certainly implies a divine intervention as we have seen in the time of Moses. Deliverance of the Jews always comes from God. If Esther does not act now, God will choose someone else.

Mordecai ends his admonition with a declaration. He firmly asserts that Esther's ascension to the royal position is "for such a time as this" (4:14). Again, the implication is that God providentially prepared Esther to be the queen of the Persian Empire so that the Jews could be saved from total annihilation. Mordecai is making himself clear. If Esther refuses to help her people, then she is not complying with God. Her disobedience is not only against Mordecai and the Jewish nation, but also God. This is not the way of virtue. Virtue always does what is right in the sight of God.

Esther's Final Decision

Esther needs to make a choice. Should she break the laws of the royal court, risking her life to make a petition for her people? Or should she break the ways of virtue and disobey God and His people to live a comfortable life as the queen of the greatest empire in the world? The latter seems much more appealing than the former. This is what people like Haman would choose to do. Esther is shrewd. She knows how the palace operates. As long as she pleases the king, she may survive this ordeal. She has done well thus far. She has gained trust and favor from the king. Why would she risk her hard-earned reputation?

By contrast, if she were to follow Mordecai's suggestion, she would have to risk everything, her queenship and life. The odds are too great. The chances are that she will be either killed or, at best, thrown into the pit of utter shame like Queen Vashti. Esther should not be hesitating here. She should join the power play and begin to live for herself. She has the ability to win favor, and no one can escape her charm, even the king. When she can use that talent for her advantage, she can be the most powerful woman of the empire. Who cares about Jewish people? As Joseph Stalin once quipped, "the death of a man is tragic but the death of a million men is trivial." What does the vast number of Jewish people have to do with Esther? Is it not beyond Esther's capacity to change the fate of the entire nation? Besides, the job of saving the whole nation belongs to the kings or gods. A young, fragile woman is a wrong person to take on this insurmountable task. Surely, Mordecai is asking too much of her.

Esther needs to make a tough choice. Indeed, she does. She sends a reply to Mordecai, saying that she will go to the king (4:16). Once again, Mordecai's counsel pushes her to the limit. This time, it has taken Esther to commit herself to a seemingly impossible task. Why is Mordecai doing this to her? Mordecai's job is to awaken Esther's virtue so that she stays on the right track. To know what we are made to do is the first step toward revealing the true virtue that lies in us. So, we all must hear the call from God and open our eyes to see our true vocation. Due to Mordecai's strong nudging, Esther now knows precisely what she must do. It is her "fate." This is her "pur." She accepts her God-given vocation and steps up to the plate where only heroes and heroines are found. The virtue has awakened indeed, and a heroine is about to emerge from the crucible of a threatened genocide.

Esther's One Last Request

She will go to the king but under one condition. She declares to Mordecai, "Go, gather together all the Jews who are in Susa, and fast for me. Do not eat or drink for three days, night or day. I and my attendants will fast as you do" (4:16). Why is she asking him and the Jews to fast for her? What does "fasting" have to do with anything? The significance of this enigmatic request from Esther does not lie in the political or cultural vignettes. If we were to say that this is politically relevant, then Esther may be seen as the one who is exploiting the symbol of "fasting" (e.g., a complete surrender) to take charge of the situation and play the role of a political leader who saves the incompetent Jews. If we were to say that this is culturally relevant, then Esther may be seen as the one who is following the cultural or religious custom to make herself pure before a possible sacrifice that she has to make for her people.

None of these explanations fit the bill. Her request for fasting may be politically and culturally relevant, but the true intent of fasting lies in her faith decision. Esther wants everyone to fast because the fate of her life and her people is in the hands of God. The matter is spiritual more so than political or cultural. Again, although God is not mentioned, Jewish people fasted not just for the sake of political or cultural purposes, but more importantly, for God. One good example is Daniel's fasting (e.g., Dan. 10:2). Fasting is normally related to praying. He fasted and prayed before the God of heaven so that he can maintain an unimpeded connection with God.

Fasting is a spiritual activity, although it involves food abstinence. Queen Esther is spiritually preparing herself before God, and as an act of prayer, she is asking God to intervene and save her and all the Jews out there. "Where does my help come from? It comes from Yahweh, the Maker of heaven and earth" (Ps. 121:1-2). Her fasting seeks the power that is beyond the power of this world. She is a true power player. She knows the source of the greatest power. It is not of the world or the king but God.

The chapter ends with Esther's final instruction: "I will go to the king, even though it is against the law. And if I perish, I perish" (4:16b). This shows that her decision is final. There is no turning back. Also, her saying, "if I perish, I perish" is the statement of her faith. She now puts her life in the hands of God. It is no longer her who decides the fate of her own life. It is up to God to either save her or not. However, this statement also has another implication. Even if God does not save her, she will still go ahead and see the king. This is a sign of the greatest virtue. Esther has completely emptied herself. There is no more "ego" that gets in her way. She is now truly free.

Virtue Lives Again

The greatest virtue is putting our life in the hands of God, whether God saves us or not. This is the faith that pleases God. Here, Esther displays the quality of "hesed" virtue. She pleases not only men but also God (Heb 11:6). I am sure that at this moment there must have been an intimate communication between Esther and God. More than likely,

God would have said to Esther, "Well done, good and faithful servant," as Esther responds, "Yahweh God, I put my life in your hands. I trust in you, my God, and I will not be disappointed. My enemies will not laugh at me" (Ps. 25:1).

Esther's determination is comparable to the faithfulness of three friends of Daniel—Shadrach, Meshach and Abednego, for they declared, "If we are thrown into the blazing furnace, the God we serve is able to deliver us from it, and he will deliver us from Your Majesty's hand. But even if he does not, we want you to know, Your Majesty, that we will not serve your gods" (Dan. 3:17-18). Esther joining the thousands of the faithful Jews and Christians declares the "even-if" faith. "Even if God does not save me, I will not bow down to the power of this world." "Even if God may not save my life, I will still follow the ways of God." "I will still follow the ways of virtue." Hallelujah!

The power from on high is upon Esther. Like Spirit-filled David who defeated Goliath, Esther is filled with the Spirit from on high. "If I perish, I perish." Such a dramatic and powerful statement must be of the Spirit. The Spirit of God who is the source of her courage is upon her. The Spirit of God who came upon Jesus to fulfill the vocation of the Suffering Servant (e.g., Isa 53) for the world, is upon her. The Spirit of God who came upon Stephen before his death boldly declaring God's word to the religious leaders, is upon her. The Spirit of God is upon her to defeat the enemy that is trying to devour her people. Who can be against us if God is for us? (Rom. 8:31).

Chapter 5

The Transformation of Virtue

After three days of fasting, Esther goes to the king. By doing this, she has stepped outside the boundary of the palace law, and not only that, she is trying to accomplish the unthinkable—i.e., overturning the unalterable. Can she really reverse the king's decree? Does not the whole kingdom rest on the unalterable words of the king? How can a mere young lass tear down the unchangeable? The odds are surely against her. However, regardless of the odds, she is determined to go ahead with the impossible mission.

In this respect, she stands tall with the guild of missionaries who risk their lives to save the lost. Even today, there are thousands of God's precious servants who are going to the unknown territories just to preach the gospel to the unreached people around the world, though the odd of success is always against them. I can almost hear their cries of pain and suffering, as they encounter extreme difficulties. We must admire their courage. Without courage, true transformation cannot occur as in the case of Esther.

Esther's Beauty, Courage, and Prayer

She is wearing a royal robe. Her beauty matches her colorful and exuberant wardrobe. She shines brightly like a lighthouse in the dark of the night. Only the blind will not be able to see her. She is so conspicuous that the king is sure to take notice of her.

Her boldness is breathtaking. She refuses to cringe and hide behind the royal officials. She makes herself a target that no one can miss. Her courage is truly admirable. She is like a firefighter, who runs into the blazing fire and pulls out a dying man, even though he knows that the fire might consume him as well as the victim. Surely, sacrificial courage must be another key sign of virtue.

She stands "in the inner court of the palace, in front of the king's hall" (5:1). Though her courage has led her to this moment, she must be trembling, knowing the lethal danger of appearing before Xerxes without first being summoned. If she loses the king's "favor," she is done. Everything hangs on this moment. Even the most courageous hero cannot but tremble in times like this. We can only pray. "Dear God, let your hand of mercy be upon her. Let your mercy flow like a river. Let her see the glory of your deliverance, one more time."

A desperate time like this calls for a desperate prayer. Nehemiah prayed to God just before he made his request to the king. He wanted to ask the king to rebuild the temple and the city wall of Jerusalem, but knowing that the chances of having his voice heard are slim, he prayed to God quickly before petitioning the king (Neh. 2:1-4). Like Nehemiah, Esther probably prayed a quick prayer for God's intervention. Indeed, it is time for a divine supernatural intervention, for no one is greater or more powerful than the great king of Persia, Xerxes, except God.

The King's Pardon and Esther's Prudence

At last, the king takes notice of her. He is pleased to see the queen and extends his golden scepter (5:2). She is saved! She wants to let out shouts of joy, or at least a deep sigh, but she cannot. She must be cautious and act prudently. Her every move counts. She cannot mess up. So much is on the line. Indeed, courage must be accompanied by prudence. Proverbs 12:33 says, "A prudent man conceals knowledge, but the heart of fools proclaim folly." In other words, prudence is connected to wisdom. A wise person is cautious and tames the overcharged emotion and this is precisely what Esther is doing. She is as wise as she is virtuous.

In 5:2, the Hebrew word "hen" reappears. It shows that Esther continues to retain the king's "favor" even though she has not seen him for the last 30 days (4:11b). It is another evidence that Esther's virtue is genuine. Her virtue, beauty, and wisdom please the king so much that the king is willing to give her "up to half the kingdom" (5:3). The king who is himself wise and prudent in his own way knows that Esther is special. However, there is a catch. Even though he says that he would share his kingdom with Esther, had Esther rashly accepted the offer, Xerxes would have quickly shifted his gear and made Esther another target of his power play. Esther's sharp intelligence avoids this pitfall and turns to a less "demanding" offer. She is exhibiting the legendary prudence of a sage.

Another Banquet

Judiciously, Esther requests her king to attend a banquet that she has prepared for him, together with Haman (5:4). It is a small request compared to asking for a share of his kingdom. Who can resist good food, music, entertainment, and wine with a beautiful wife and his viceroy? The king does not hesitate and orders Haman to come to the banquet. After the banquet, the king asks, "What is your petition?" The king knows that Esther's private party means something more. He knows instinctively that Esther wants something from him. As he has already pointed out, he is willing to give almost everything. In spite of that, Esther defers her petition to tomorrow. Again, she simply asks the king and Haman to come to the banquet tomorrow.

Esther's deferment puts the king on high suspense. The king's curiosity must have peaked by now. Esther is trying to say something to him, but she is not. What is it? It must have stoked his interest. The stake is higher now. The king's interest has climaxed. Esther must give the king her answer by tomorrow. A new hurdle appears. How can she break the news and convince the king that Haman is the villain and she and her people are his victims? What would make the king choose her rather than his faithful viceroy? What kind of a business deal can she make with the king to save her people? It seems that Esther is not out of the woods yet.

Haman's Folly

By contrast, Haman is in good spirits, humming to himself as he returns to his home (5:9). He sees Mordecai at the king's gate, but Mordecai again refuses to stand up and bow before him. His good mood is quickly spoiled by Mordecai's inflexibility. Haman is filled with rage, but he does nothing to him. Perhaps, he does not want Mordecai's blood on his hands, but more likely, it is due to his cowardice. He may not have the decency or the courage to stand up to Mordecai. He may have feared that Mordecai could strike him dead on the spot, even though there are guards around. Regardless, he just leaves Mordecai behind and goes back to his home.

Haman's folly is discernible as he gathers his friends and Zeresh, his wife, to tell them how great he is, having a rank higher than everyone else (5:11). His arrogance skyrockets as he interprets Esther's invitation to her banquet as the recognition of his highest honor in the kingdom next only to the king. All this does not make him happy though. He is absolutely furious about Mordecai. So the wisdom of his wife, Zeresh, suggests a new scheme to Haman. She asks him to build a hanging pole so high that everyone can see Mordecai's impalement.

Haman and the gang laugh together, celebrating their wealth and power. They laugh at the expense of someone else's misery. This is what the power of the world does to people. Power and glory in this world drive people to be greedy, self-centered, and oppressive. They become dull and insensitive to the pain and suffering of others. The Golden Rule does not apply to them. The weak, the marginalized, and the needy are beyond them. The blessings that they have are rarely shared. Wealth and power are non- negotiable. Anything or anyone who does not bow to the power that they have will be cut down like an unwanted tree in the street.

Jesus came and saw this injustice taking place in his own time. He spoke to the Pharisees. "Whoever is the greatest should be the servant of the others. If you put yourself above others, you will be put down. But if you humble yourself, you will be honored" (Mat. 23:11-12). This is the new logic of God's kingdom. God's kingdom does not operate based on the rules or the game played by the power mongrels. It is based on true humbleness. Is this not what virtue is all about, the greatest becoming the servant of the lowest? If the world is to be renewed, we must keep this rule of virtue alive.

Chapter 6

Mordecai and Haman, Who is Greater?

The night before the second banquet that Esther had prepared for the king, a small yet significant event takes place in the palace. The king is restless. He is not able to sleep. Perhaps, Esther's strange behavior is bothering him. The Bible does not give us enough details, but it is likely that the king is extremely excited and at the same time intrigued by Esther. He cannot wait to see what is waiting for him tomorrow at the banquet.

To kill time, he reads the book of the chronicles (6:1). The book of the chronicles is not exactly an entertaining book filled with the stories of adventures. Rather, it is a long historical record of the king's deeds, accomplishments, and sayings, along with major occurrences that are related to his ruling. Since Xerxes already knows most of the things he did, reading the chronicle should have been a boring exercise.

However, in the ancient times, kings often checked the book of the chronicles to ensure that their deeds and accomplishments are well preserved and properly noted. These royal tyrants want to make sure that all their accomplishments are properly recorded. Hence, checking the book of the chronicles is not trivial but an important part of the king's life.

Honoring a Hero

As he was flipping the pages, he soon realizes that Mordecai had exposed an assassination plot and saved his life. This is no small matter. One of the key factors for the power play is the preservation of the throne. To preserve the throne, the king's life must be protected at all costs. To take the throne, often ruthless men resort to killing the king. The Bible records several instances in which these killings had occurred (e.g., 2 Kings). Since Mordecai prevented such a devastation for the king, Xerxes needs to reward him, but he cannot remember whether he did anything for Mordecai. The book of the chronicles is silent in that respect.

He asks his attendants, "What honor and recognition has Mordecai received for this" (6:3)? His attendants come back with a simple answer, "Nothing." A frustrated look on the king's face is inevitable. How can this be? Nothing has been done to a hero of the kingdom. Is not saving a king the greatest act of all? He gets up and shouts. "Who is in the court" (6:4)? He looks for a royal official who can take the king's message to Mordecai. Incidentally, Haman, the king's viceroy is standing in the court. He was there to "speak to the king about impaling Mordecai on the pole he had set up for him" (6:4b).

Xerxes and Haman once again are having a face- to-face meeting. This time, it is the king who wants Haman's service to honor Mordecai. What a paradox!

Just a few days ago, Xerxes and Haman met together to conspire against the Jews, and the king agreed to eradicate all the Jews once and for all. Certainly, Mordecai also belongs to the same fate as other Jews for he cannot escape Haman's treacherous plot. In this occasion, however, they are meeting to discuss the heroic act of Mordecai. Of course, Haman does not know that the king is talking about Mordecai. The paradox continues with an odd combination of events.

First, the king without identifying the man of honor asks Haman, "What should be done for the man the king delights to honor" (6:6)? There is no reason for the king to hide the name of the man that he wants to honor here. Right away, Xerxes should have spilled out the name and told Haman that he wants to honor Mordecai. However, the king does not mention the name to Haman. Did this paradox happen because of a simple mishap on the part of the king? The story is too tightly related to other events to be treated as a simple royal blunder. Rather, such an occasion is timed and organized by a divine intervention, for "in all things God works for the good of those who love him" (Rom 8:28).

Second, Haman jumps to a wrong conclusion, thinking to himself, "Who is there that the king would rather honor than me?" and hastily responds to this intriguing question posed by the king:

For the man the king delights to honor, have them bring a royal robe the king has worn and a horse the king has ridden, one with a royal crest placed on its head. Then let the robe and horse be entrusted to one of the king's most noble princes. Let them robe the man the king delights to honor and lead him on the horse through the city streets, proclaiming before him, "This is what is done for the man the king delights to honor" (6:7–9).

Such a dramatic request has never been done before. No one has the power or authority to wear the king's robe, ride the king's horse, and place a royal crest on its head. This is prescribed only to the king. Had such an honor been given to a man, that man would be considered equal to the king. Indeed, it would be the greatest honor that the king can give to a man.

This is not all. The man to be honored is to be robed by the king's most noble prince and led on the horse through the city streets, proclaiming the honor of the man. Once again, only the king is privileged to have such a magnificent public display. Even the king himself is not robed by the most noble prince every day. Only on a special occasion, such as the celebration of winning a war against the greatest foe of the empire, can the king be robed by the most noble prince in the kingdom. On a daily basis, his attendants or servants robe him.

Likewise, the most noble prince does not lead the horse and proclaim the deeds of the man on the horse going throughout the city streets. That vocation is reserved for the king's attendants. Such a visible gesture on the part of the royal prince is a clear sign that the man on the horse has the honor and respect that is only equal to the king, if not, more than the king.

In this respect, Haman's recommendations are incredible. It can only be contrived by a man who wants to have the highest honor for himself. Haman mistakenly interprets the king's request and surmises quickly that the man of honor that the king is talking about is him. This is Haman's greatest folly. In contrast to Esther's prudence and wisdom, Haman's folly is distinguishable as he is thinking only about himself.

The King's Odd Behavior

What is more incredible is that the king takes Haman's advice. King Xerxes, the one who neither shares his honor nor exalts anyone else, has permitted Haman to carry out this stunning recommendation given to the king. Why would he do that? Is he not a man who cares about nothing but himself? Is he not a man who does not share his honor with anyone else? It does not make sense for him to honor a man as such, though he has done a great service to the king.

There is no known explanation for the king's odd behavior. However, thinking deeply about the whole incident, we can discern that the king has been changed. He has turned from a ruthless tyrant to a merciful king. What has changed him? His heart has been changed because of Esther's virtuous influence upon his life. Virtue changes people. It brings joy when there is no joy. It brings lasting godly pleasure when there is only worldly pleasure that is fleeting more quickly than the summer rain. It soothes and heals the broken hearts. Esther is the source of the king's healing power.

The king is in a good and generous mood. His sleepless night has to do with the excitement from Esther's banquet. The king probably knew that Queen Esther had risked her life to stand before him—a rare display of humility and respect from a queen to the king. Esther's honorable act contrasts well with Queen Vashti's disobedience. Moreover, Esther honored the king's name before his second-in-command by holding a special feast for him. Esther praised and exalted the king before the most competent viceroy of the kingdom, firmly establishing the royal reputation for the world to see. What more can he ask from a queen?

Haman's Cowardice

The turn of events does not end here. As we know, Haman's recommendation is given to the king because Haman thought that the king was honoring him. Who else could have such an honor other than himself? Given the opportunity, he asks the king the things that no man ever could have so that he could puff up his pride and ego as far as he can take it. He had no idea that the king wanted to honor his archenemy, Mordecai. Suddenly, the king orders Haman to carry out the recommended plan and tells him to lead the man of honor, who is Mordecai.

What a shock! "Mordecai!" With eyes wide open, Haman looks at the king, but soon realizes that the king has in mind Mordecai all along. He could vent his frustration and confront the king. "Why are you doing this to me?" "Don't you know Mordecai is a Jew?" "You were supposed to kill him!" "Why are you honoring him instead of me?" He could throw a fit and rebel against the king, but Haman is no man of valor. He is a coward. Unlike Esther, he does not put himself in harm's way for any cause. Haman having no other choice but to carry out the king's order takes the robe and the horse and leads Mordecai on horseback through the city square, shouting, "This is what is done for the man the king delights to honor!"

How humiliating it is for Haman! Haman returns to his home, and this time, it is Haman's turn to wail and put ashes on his head. In the first round, Mordecai was defeated, but in the second round, it is Haman who lost the fight. Haman, who is not used to losing fights, now faces the tragic reality. How could he lose the fight against Mordecai, a simple Jewish peasant? His ego and pride are certainly crushed. What is more interesting is that Mordecai had not even moved a finger or planned an elaborate scheme to win the battle against Haman. Because of a series of turns and twists, Mordecai emerges as the victor of this battle without laying a single finger on Haman. In this respect, Jesus is right. "Those who exalt themselves will be humbled and those who humble themselves will be exalted" (Mat. 23:12). This is the principle of virtue. Virtue and pride are two opposing forces, the former brings honor and the latter dishonor. What is honorable surely overpowers what is dishonorable.

Mordecai's Delayed Honor

God's timing is perfect. Mordecai's honor has been deferred to this day for a reason. It had a higher purpose. Its purpose is to show that the wicked will be humbled, and the humble will be exalted. This is the key principle of the kingdom of God. Only the humble and the meek belong to the kingdom of God. This is the core teaching of Jesus (e.g., Mat 5:5). Besides, had Mordecai been recognized at the wrong time, he would never have received the most magnificent display of honor in the Persian Empire.

We look for an immediate result and urge God, "Where are you? Why have you forsaken me? Why are you silent when I am mistreated and dismissed in this world? Please, make things happen for me now!" Surely, God is silent in many instances. However, His silence does not mean that He has forgotten about us. Rather, His silence means that He is waiting for the right time for His deliverance. As the fisherman waits for the right time so that he can catch the best fish, God waits for the optimal time so that in all things He can work for the good of those who love Him.

The Beginning of Haman's Downfall

Haman goes back to his home and gathers his advocates, including his wife. It is time for him to come out with a bang. He must give all he has to finish off Mordecai. A revenge is in order. Mordecai must pay for the humiliation Haman received today. Haman will not rest until he sees Mordecai eliminated. But strangely, Haman's friends and wife do not come up with crafty schemes anymore. Rather, they warn him: "Since Mordecai, before whom your downfall has started, is of Jewish origin, you cannot stand against him—you will surely come to ruin" (6:13).

It seems that his advisors and wife finally figured out that Haman cannot win the fight against Mordecai. There is something more than what appears to be. It seems that Haman's friends are attributing Haman's continual mishaps to Haman's own plan to eradicate Jews, including Mordecai. In other words, they are simply stating the fact that Haman started something that he should not have. Killing off the entire nation was not the right thing to do. They finally realized the horror of this act. But it is too late. Haman's demise is already here, as he is hurried away by the king's eunuchs to Esther's banquet (6:14).

Chapter 7

Esther's Victory

Esther's banquet continues to the second day. It is not unusual for the royal feast to last more than a single day. In Chapter 1, we have seen that King Xerxes displayed his wealth and power by holding a banquet that lasted seven days (1:5). But there is a difference. King Xerxes' elaborate party was for the public, whereas Esther's banquet is privately held. No one else but the king and Haman are invited. It is a time to be more intimate with each other.

While enjoying the company of his beautiful queen, King Xerxes finally pops the question that was hovering in his head for the last two days. "Esther, what is your petition?" He knows instinctively that Esther has something to say and it is slowly getting on his nerves. Had Esther deferred his question again, the king for sure would have lost his temper. It is time for Esther to take her stance and boldly face the challenge that lies ahead.

Courage and More Courage

Courage is needed once again. This time, she must be not only prudent but also eloquent so that her words do not implicate any power manipulation or exploitation from the king. Her request must signal nothing but transparency and straightforwardness. She cannot beat around the bush and expect the king to figure out what she wants. It must be clear and yet convincing.

For a young woman, this is too much to ask. In the hands of a fragile Esther lies the lives of thousands if not millions of people. One wrong move and she could slip and fall. This time, the fall will be much more severe than the fall of Queen Vashti. Esther knows the danger. She knows the consequences. She must be trembling like a lost puppy sitting on the street in the cold winter night. Nonetheless, she remains courageous.

Her courage comes not just from her prudence or intelligence. It also stems from the prayers of her people. Solidarity is stronger than fear. She knows that thousands of her people are fasting and praying for her. She knows that, through this collective fasting and prayer, God hears. The petition has already gone to heaven. Solidarity is made even stronger as God is now involved with her plan. The petition has been made to God, so she is ready now to take the next step.

Esther's Petition

Esther speaks succinctly. "Spare my people—this is my request" (7:3). She does not mince words. Her concise and brief words of petition are supported with yet another forceful short explanation. "For I and my people have been sold to be destroyed, killed and annihilated. If we had merely been sold as male and female slaves, I would have kept quiet, because no such distress would justify disturbing the king" (7:4).

Esther knows that the king does not want to hear any "distressing" news. Not now. Is not the banquet a time of singing, rejoicing, and having fun? The king is already stressed by the fact that he has to watch out for his enemies who are always lurking behind the corner to take away his kingdom. Esther's banquet provides him much needed rest and peace. To break that peace is to bash the king's spirit to pieces. It is one of the unpardonable travesties against the lord of Persian kingdom. However, pleading to the king's favor (hesed), Esther speaks of the reality of her fate. She and her people will be "destroyed, killed and annihilated." The situation is weighty enough to crash the king's banquet.

The king is disturbed. He rides an emotional roller coaster. Just a few minutes ago, he was having a good time with his queen and the viceroy. But now, he is upset. Hearing that someone is trying to kill his queen means also that there is a rebellion brewing inside his palace, a show of confrontation toward his throne. Who would dare to do such a thing? Even Xerxes did not kill his previous queen. Queen Vashti was sent away, but her life was spared. Who would go beyond him and overpower his throne and take the life of his queen and her people?

Prudence and More Prudence

Even at this point, Esther does not mention that she is a Jew. She has not identified herself as such because she knows that Xerxes may react differently had she done so. She knows that there had been an agreement between the king and Haman concerning her people. As far as the king is concerned, Jews are the source of his problem. No one has told him otherwise yet.

She wisely keeps her identity hidden. There is no need for her to provoke the king and reveal her Jewish origin. She cannot be the target now. She has to let the king focus on Haman and his evil deeds against the queen and her people. For this reason, Esther makes sure that the king understands the problem. The problem is not the Jews but the one who is trying to kill the queen of Persia and threatening the throne of the king.

Without hesitation, the king wants a name. "Who is he, and where is he?" "Who dares to do this?" Esther looks at Haman and raises her voice. "A foe and enemy, this wicked Haman" (7:6). The verdict is out, finally. Esther now names the true enemy of Persia, and he is Haman-the-Wicked. The king is now furious. He has lost his temper and he is unable to stand still. His hand is shaking. His face is wrapped up in anger. His wrath is about to be poured out upon Haman.

Haman's Final Folly

Xerxes steps out to the palace garden to cool himself down, but Haman does not follow the king. Had he done so he could have explained the situation from his point of view. But once again, he is too afraid. He is afraid that the angry king will kill him on site. His life is hanging by the thread, and ironically, the only person who can save him is none other than Esther, the one who he was trying to kill. The dramatic effect of reversal is taking place. The cat that chased the mouse is now on his knees, asking the mouse to spare his life. What a change of fortune! The enemy is at her feet pleading for his life.

In desperation, Haman throws himself on the couch where Esther is sitting (7:8). He is terrified. Fear takes over him. He extends his hand to take hold of Esther. His intention is to hold onto her like a drowning man trying to grab whatever he can to save his life. However, Haman is too late. His fate has already been decided. This is his "pur." There is nothing he can do. In fact, the matter gets worse. At this very moment, the king comes back and sees Haman trying to grab Esther. King Xerxes interprets Haman's desperate measure as an attempt to "assault the queen" in his presence (7:8). Haman is immediately taken away.

There is no need to find further evidence of Haman's wrongdoing. The king has decided already. A crime scene is conveniently provided by Haman himself. Although Haman had no intention of "assaulting" the queen right then and there, it is wrong for Haman to approach the queen in the way he did. It is surely a sign of imprudence. Haman's sloppy behavior once again digs a deeper hole for him. His lack of virtue throws him into the pit of everlasting doom.

Haman's Erased Identity

Haman's face is covered before he is taken away by the palace attendants and soldiers, as if he no longer has an identity (7:8). His existence is now over. His legacy and achievements have been blotted out. He has been defaced and shamed. He is being treated as the enemy of the land. He is not just any enemy but a betrayer. He has betrayed the trust of the king and the queen. Instead of working for the empire, he has decided to divide and destroy the land, first by trying to kill innocent people, and in doing so, the queen of Persia, all because of his arrogance and pride.

Pride is the seat of evil. It is the antithesis of virtue. Virtue's two main companions are humility and self- sacrifice. Virtue does not want to hurt others for the sake of one's own selfish gain. Virtue does not conspire to take the lives of innocent men. Rather, virtue suffers with those who are in pain. It creates a spiritual solidarity with those who are suffering. And because of it, it brings hope to the marginalized. It allows the good, just, and the beauty to survive in the most deplorable places.

Harbona, one of the king's eunuchs, offers an immediate sentencing for the crimes committed by Haman. "Look, the very gallows that Haman has prepared for Mordecai, whose word saved the king, stands at Haman's house, fifty cubits high" (7:9). Harbona is doing several things by giving this advice to the king. First, Harbona is stating that Haman's crime is extensive, for Haman also tries to kill Mordecai who is a hero that saved the king's life from the assassins. Second, Harbona is exposing Haman's gallows, which are unlawful to build without the king's permission. Only the king's law and his decree can convict a man to be killed. Third, Harbona speaks of Haman's arrogance as the gallows are built so high, extending to 50 cubits. Who can dare to build such monstrous gallows in the middle of the king's city unless that person's pride is higher than that of the king?

The Death of Haman

At last, Haman meets his fate. He is hung on the gallows he made in his house. Haman faces a horrible death. His despicable and ugly life is capped with the death that no one wants to talk about. Such a man is shunned by the public, for anyone hung on a tree is under God's curse (Deut. 21:23). Because of the gallows being so high, all passersby in the city must have seen him hanging on the pole. It is the utmost shameful death. This is the death of a criminal. The people standing by spit at him. They taunt him for what he did. They speak the words of a curse so that the curse may all be on the criminal and nothing is left behind for the living community.

Such a death reminds us of the death of Jesus Christ. He died on the cross. He was raised up high. It was the most shameful death. It was the most painful death. People taunted Him. They mocked Him. They cursed Him. They spit at Him. But unlike Haman, Jesus was not a criminal. He did not deserve such an excruciating death. Why did He die such a shameful, painful death? It is because of our sins. In place of us who are sinners like Haman the Wicked, He sacrificed His life so that we can have life that belongs to Him. This is the stunning revelation of the love of God. Because God so loved us, He sent His only begotten son so that we may not go through the shameful, painful death on the cross, but have life, and have it to the fullest. Jesus' true act of virtue has saved us all.

In this respect, virtue has two sides. It is ugly as well as beautiful. It is ugly insofar as it embraces the ugliness of this world such as sin and injustice. However, it is ultimately beautiful since it transforms the ugliness into something precious and glorious. In the Book of Esther, through the virtuousness of our heroes, the ugliness of evil, curses, and death is diffused and turned into the beauty of goodness, justice, and everlasting bliss.

The duality of virtue also integrates the humbleness of common life and the exotic life of royalty. Virtue takes what is trivial and ordinary and raises its bar so high that what is trivial and ordinary turns into what is exotic and grandiose so much so that it deserves to be recognized by all. The Psalmist has realized this already and states that, "[God] raises the poor from the dust and lifts the needy from the ash heap; he seats them with princes, with the princes of his people" (Ps 113:8). Behind such a leap of status lies the God-given virtue that is ready to please God and transform the world.

Chapter 8

Esther Saves the Jews

The battle has been fought and the lady of victory is on Esther's side. Esther, Mordecai, and all the Jews survive the threat of genocide. Through the turn of fortune instigated by the virtuous acts of Esther and Mordecai, the Jews emerge from the grave once again. Haman, who is now called "the enemy of the Jews" (8:1) is forever perished. Ironically, the persecutors are persecuted, and the defeated became the victors.

The Defeated Are the Victors

In Esther's paradigm, those who lose win. The arrogant reveling of those in power is supplanted by the lowly and the humble. As an example, Haman's proud possession, his own house, is taken away from him. King Xerxes gives it to

Esther. It is the trophy of the victor. What belongs to the enemy now belongs to the victor. Perhaps, Xerxes recognizes the fact that the battle had taken place between the kingdom of Persia and its betrayer, Haman. This battle was as important as any other battle he fought. Had he lost the battle, he would have lost not only his queen but also his reputation, for he allowed his second-in- command to take away his queen before his very eyes.

However, the battle is less about the Persian Empire than the Jewish nation. The fierce battle that Esther fought was not for the Persian Empire, but for her people, the Jews. For this reason, verse 8:1 specially mentions that Haman, not the Persian Empire, is the "enemy of the Jews." It was Haman who planned to destroy the innocent Jews just because his ego was damaged by Mordecai's unyielding attitude toward him.

The Law and the King

Ironically, Xerxes was in on it too. He gladly agreed with Haman to destroy the Jews and sent off his approval to every corner of the empire. However, the Bible is silent about Xerxes. It does not call him an "enemy of the Jews." Rather, he is portrayed as one of the key agents who helped Esther preserve her people from an impending doom.

What we need to understand is that Xerxes is represented in the Bible as the standing law of a nation. As we all know, the law plays a vital role in the sustenance and maintenance of society. If it's corrupt, it destroys not only the society's order, but more importantly, the grassroots who are at the mercy of those who have power over them. If the law functions properly, it brings social balance. It is an equalizer that affirms, "All men are created equal," regardless of sex, race, or economic status. In order to set the law on the right tract, virtue is needed. Virtue is the guiding light that unveils justice and truth to the law-givers and law-keepers.

Although virtue is the law's guiding light, it does not suspend the law; rather, it works within the frame of the given social structure. The main task of virtue is to identify the source of evil so that the law can properly function in its role of eradicating the vice of our society and transform it into something that is good, just, and beautiful.

Xerxes is now on the right track. He is guided by virtue. He is no longer in the dark being hypnotized by the power of evil. He now sees clearly. His eyes are no longer blinded by the false claims of his servants. He knows what is right and what is wrong. Esther catches this tiny breakthrough in the king's attitude. It is now a good time for her to disclose Mordecai's identity.

Esther's Final Request

Esther tells the king that Mordecai is "related to her" (8:1b). Xerxes knows well that he was the one who saved his life. Esther introduces to the king this "well- known" hero. By her introduction, Esther gains Xerxes' trust even more and the king feels secure since he is surrounded by a trusted family.

The king asks no other question. He recognizes the virtue and honor of Mordecai and Esther, so he takes off his signet ring and gives it to Mordecai. It was given to Haman but now it belongs to Mordecai. The power has found a new owner, a man of virtue.

Esther's work is not yet done. There is another key task remaining. Although Haman is dead, the Jewish people are still in danger. Because of the irrevocable king's edict that has been sent out already, the lives of the Jews are like the candles in the wind. She has to save them. However, in order to save them, she has to go before the king once again, without a proper summon. This is always a risky business. As we have seen, without the king's proper summon, no one is to approach the king. Only the extension of the king's golden scepter revokes this requirement.

For the last time, Esther does not hesitate to go to the king's court and drops to the floor in tears. She pleads to the king to "avert the evil design of Haman" (8:3). If the king does not rescind the decree he had written against the Jews, it would be devastating to her people. Perhaps, Esther may be saved by a special decree of the king. Perhaps, Mordecai may be saved too because of what he did for the king and his relationship to the queen. However, that is not enough for Esther. Esther keeps her virtue and once again risks her life for the many.

Esther's Identity Revealed

Here, without hesitation, Esther reveals her hidden identity (8:6). Prior to this moment, Esther has not mentioned to the king that she was a Jew. But now, she unveils her true identity. She tells the truth despite the possible political repercussions. The boldness of Esther is at its highest point. Because of it, Esther now recovers her lost identity, and unlike Haman, whose act of injustice and cowardice made him lose his identity and life, the innocent and submissive Esther gains a new identity, a daring and subversive heroic Jew.

The king, at last, holds out his scepter to Esther. He commands, "You may write as you please with regard to the Jews, in the name of the king, and seal it with the king's ring; for an edict written in the name of the king and sealed with the king's ring cannot be revoked" (8:8). Here, Xerxes sounds like God, speaking the words that cannot be revoked. The king's secretaries are summoned, and a new edict is sent to every province. A new power is given to the Jews. "By these letters the king allowed the Jews who were in every city to assemble and defend their lives, to destroy, to kill, and to annihilate any armed force of any people or province that might attack them" (8:11). It is an unprecedent event. Nowhere in the history of Persia had the Jews been given power to arm and defend themselves.

Jews Fighting the Enemy

On the thirteenth day of the twelfth month, which is the month of Adar, the Jewish people come together and take revenge on their enemies (8:13–14). The victory belongs to the Jews. At last, they have won the battle. This victory is a direct result of Esther's victory over Haman. Actually, the victory of the Jews stems from the virtuous acts of Esther and Mordecai, their undeterred determination and courage to save their people.

Virtue transmits God's blessing to the world. It does not work for the sake of its own gain. It is shared, and as it shares, it grows ever greater for all to enjoy. As a result, "In every province and in every city, wherever the king's command and his edict came, there was gladness and joy among the Jews, a festival and a holiday" (8:17).

Purim, a Jewish Feast

This celebration is now called "Purim" (9:26). It is a "Jewish holiday that commemorates the saving of the Jewish people from Haman, who was planning to kill all the Jews." It has turned into a grand and flamboyant Jewish holiday.

Purim evokes laughter, erasing the violence of the kingdom. The brief explosion of freedom during this time diffuses the restrictions of royal decrees. The tears of yesterday have turned into the merry-making laughter and festivity of today. The accent is set on peripeteia, on some felicitous turn of fortune. Also, during this time of celebration, people freely exchange food and gifts. Perhaps, the exchange of gifts symbolizes the change of fate between Haman and Mordecai.

They also remember the poor and donate charity for the needy as God has remembered the insignificant Jews in the days of King Xerxes. This grand feast is topped off with the most impressive holiday carnival. Hundreds of people wear their costumes and display colorful wardrobes, face paintings, and disguises, parading through the main streets where every citizen of the town can see. It too symbolizes both Esther's glory and Mordecai's honor. The festival clearly represents remembrance of the past (the deliverance under Esther and Mordecai), but its fantasy reaches toward the future, not just in terms of the repetition of the celebration year after year, but in terms of hope and faith that, indeed, the salvation itself is perennial.

The Exchange of Pur

Indeed, the fate has turned. Instead of the Jewish diaspora that was supposed to be destroyed, Haman the royal viceroy of the Persian Empire had taken the

fall. The evil scheme of the Jewish enemies has been foiled by Esther and Mordecai. Glory be to God! The credit goes to Esther and Mordecai and their display of virtue. Without prudence, courage, and willingness to die for the people, there would not have been any celebration.

If we are a bit more careful, a bit more courageous, and a bit more affectionate for the underprivileged and marginalized, the world we know may have more shouts of celebration than the sound of dirges. If we can tame our greed and arrogance and allow virtue to reveal its true color to the world, then there would be more sounds of joy than weeping and wailing. If we love God with all our heart and our neighbors as our own selves, love would not be a rare commodity in this world. Joy, happiness, love, and mercy would be the most well- defined, most sought-after, and most-valued commodity in this world instead of gold and silver. Where are thou, O Virtue?

Chapter 9

The Wrath of God

The two final chapters of Esther seem like an addendum to the book. They retell the story of Haman's fate and the victory of the Jews. The addition to the original account, which is denoted in the previous chapter, is not extensive. It simply includes a slightly more expanded account of the Jews fighting against their enemies. Because the Jews now have an upper hand over their enemies, their victory is given.

The Jewish Advantage

It is "easy" for the Jews to identify their enemies, thanks to the king's first edict. Although the first edict could have been a devastating blow to the Jewish existence, it turns out to be good for them after all.

It becomes the key identifier of anti-Semitists and Haman protagonists. Like King Jehu of Israel who faked his allegiance to Baal worshippers in order for him to round up all Baal followers to eradicate them (2 Kings 10:28), the king's first edict functioned as the summon that named all the enemies of the Jews.

The Jews in Susa killed five hundred men. They also killed ten sons of Haman. On the thirteenth day of Adar, the total number of the Jewish enemies killed exceeds seventy-five thousand. On the fourteenth day, another three hundred are killed without anyone taking the spoils. Because so many people died, it is also a day of mourning. To the Jews, it is a day of celebration; however, to the enemy of the Jews, it is a day of condemnation. How can a single event carry such two extreme conditions?

The Duality of the Cross

It is the same with the weight of the cross. To some, it is a display of God's salvation. To some, it is a display of God's curse. To some, it is a display of God's vulnerability. To some, it is a display of God's power over death. The duality of God's work cannot be underestimated. In this world, every celebration has a dark side. It carries a joyful reminder, and at the same time, a sad ending for those who could not join the celebration.

Behind the celebration, there is a wrath of God. The wrath of God waits silently as a lion stealthily keeps hidden until the right time for its attack on the prey. Although the wicked may seem prosperous at times, eventually they will meet their demise. The celebration does not belong to them. The final celebration belongs to those who are in God. His kingdom will come, and His enemies will be rounded up and thrown "into the darkness, where there will be weeping and gnashing of teeth" (Mat 8:12).

The wrath of God is directed to those who are against Him. His enemies will not be spared. They will be blotted out from the book of life (Ps. 69:28). The sad thing is that His enemies continue to rebel against Him and add more to their guilt. It fuels the fire and makes God's wrath burn ever greater. His fire will consume His enemies without sparing their lives. Knowing the work of God's hand of judgment, we ought to magnify Him and give thanks for His mercy for sparing our lives through Jesus' precious sacrificial death on the cross. In this respect, the cross represents the endless interplay of death and renewal.

Weep for the Lost

It is interesting to note that during the celebration of Purim, the Jewish people gather together in the synagogue and read the Book of Esther. At this time, they hold up a noisy grager and drown the name of Haman whenever his name is read. They are essentially blotting out the name of their enemy so that his existence is made meaningless in the history of the Jewish nation. Moreover, a strange custom of burning an effigy of Haman turns out to be one of the highlights of Purim.

In the same way, God's wrath ends the legacy of the wicked. Whereas His faithful servants inherit His kingdom and have life to the fullest, His enemies will be forever erased and sent to the fiery lake (Mark 9:48). They will be committed to the pits of darkness in which they will be tormented. They may ask for a taste of water by dipping the tip of a finger in water and cooling off their tongue, but no one will be able to help them (Luke 16:24). Such a devastation is reserved for the enemy of God. How tragic it is!

Let those who weep, weep for the lost. Let those who shout, shout for the lost. Let those who can fight, fight for the lost. The time is coming when the gates of heaven will be shut. There will be no one to weep for the lost anymore.

Chapter 10

Mordecai's Glory

As there is a punishment for sin, there is a reward for God's virtue. Mordecai who not only stood up against Haman, but also worked tirelessly to guide Esther to the "right" direction is finally promoted to the "second in rank to King Xerxes" (10:3a). He is also held in "high esteem by his many fellow Jews, because he worked for the good of his people and spoke up for the welfare of all the Jews" (10:3b). Mordecai's virtue shines brightly as the source of all- annihilation (e.g., evil and the past pain) and all- renewal (the change of fortune for the Jews).

Virtue's Characteristics

The function of God-given virtue is similar to that of God's law. God's law guides our lives since it is "a lamp for [our] feet, a light on [our] path" (Ps. 119:05). As we are reminded again, virtue as a guiding light shines most brightly in the darkest places. Thus, virtue breaks down the power of darkness when it is most rampant. No darkness, hopelessness, or sorrow can overcome the light. Though it may not shine its light right away, eventually, in the end, God's glory will be revealed through virtue in such a way that the world of darkness may flee from it in seven ways.

Furthermore, virtue has the power to change "pur" (fate). Mordecai and his people were destined to die. The king had issued an edict that was irrevocable. The Jews had no way of freeing themselves from the death trap set up by Haman-the-Wicked. However, virtue was able to transcend the insuperable. Against all odds, Mordecai trumped his formidable enemy with his "bare hands." Though God is not "actively" intervening in the affairs of Jewish people, virtue has become God's instrument with which He raises His servants to do great things for His kingdom.

Mordecai's Glory

In Chapter 8, Mordecai's glorious appearance is visible. He wears "royal garments of blue and white, a large crown of gold and a purple robe of fine linen" (8:15). He no longer dons the commoners' attire nor the sackcloth and ashes.

He now wears his royal robe that is far more glorious than any other wardrobe in the world. Unlike the short-lived honor of Chapter 3, his newly donned attire is permanent. As the cowl makes the monk, his attire identifies the glorified nature of Mordecai. Once he was tormented and humiliated, but now, he ascends to the highest position within the royal court. His rank as well as his fate have been turned into a glorious end. This is the peripeteia of virtue. Virtue changes our "pur" of death to the life in God's glory.

Though the "pur" (lot) has been thrown by Haman, in the hands of virtue, the "pur" (fate) shows a new beginning. He is now the "great man." Only the true great man is hesed (favored). He shows kindness to his people without abusing power like that of Haman. For this reason, he is "beloved" by the public. He is not like other powerful men who are normally oppressive, egotistic, and violent. Rather, as a ruler, he serves his people, stooping down to their level and developing a mutually enriching relationship between the powerful royalties and the lowly peasants. At last, virtue has done it job of balancing the exalted with the lowlies.

Epilogue

God's glory is made up of His precious jewels, or what I call "attributes." Like a crown ornamented with precious jewels, God's glory is adorned with many precious jewels such as love, hope, faith, courage, justice, prudence, and long-suffering. As the image- bearers of God, we must endeavor to keep them as our most valued treasures and continue to reciprocate the reigning glory of God. Besides, without them, we cannot claim wholeheartedly, "O God, our Lord, how majestic is your name in all the earth, who have displayed your splendor above the heavens!" (Ps. 8:1).

Virtue is sustained by God's glory and its concomitant attributes. Without them, virtue is not really virtue at all. It can never be genuine. The reverse is also true. Virtue gives off the light of love, hope, faith, courage, justice, goodness, beauty, prudence, and long-suffering. These positive attributes form the foundation of virtue. If we follow the ways of virtue, we will see these attributes strewn on its path, and in the end, we will meet God's glory beckoning at the end of the road.

Therefore, we need to move out of the darkness of this world and find the light of God's salvation. God is calling us. "O virtue, where are thou?" God is seeking the lost. He is looking for His virtuous ones but cannot find them. He calls out but no one answers (e.g., Song 5:6). At last, He shines upon this dark and gloomy world with the light of Christ, signaling to all just to come, whether virtuous or not (Mat. 22:10). If we are not virtuous anymore, we can be "made" virtuous by the light of Christ and His precious sacrifice on the cross. So, the final message from God is to come and drink from the well of Jesus Christ and let the Spirit of His love adorn us with the attributes of godly virtue. Our ultimate goal is then to come and partake in the banquet that God has prepared for us.

However, despite God's calling, the world likes to remain in darkness, where virtue cannot be found easily. The opening act of Esther shows that the world is full of intoxicated, power-hungry, and intolerant people who determine their own fate as well as others based on compulsive behaviors and insatiable greed. The world's system runs on the engine which is fueled by self-indulgence and self-gratification. To keep it running perpetually and without any glitch, anything that impedes the promotion of greed is cut down mercilessly. This is precisely what happened in the palace of the Persian Empire.

Haman's wickedness proves the point. Haman had no virtue in his life. He planned a horrifying genocide just to get rid of a non-conforming Jew. How can anyone think of such a thing? It is because virtue was no longer the reigning queen in his life. It was his ego that stood aloof. Nothing could stand before it. It was non-negotiable and non-compromising. It was the absolute.

Perhaps, in Haman's life, this was not the case always. When he was a child, he may have been virtuous, doing good things to others, helping out his family, and sacrificing his time and effort for the sake of the community to which he belonged. However, even if we claim that he was virtuous when he was a young lad, we know that Haman acted wickedly as an adult. Evidently, he went on with his life without any regard for virtue. What changed him? At one point in his life, he probably realized that nature is armed with teeth and claws. In order to survive and be on top, he needed to be more vicious than nature. So he chose to be wicked without any regard for virtue. He climbed the ladder, rising above all other political ranks, thanks to setting virtue aside and doing wicked things in his life. Perhaps, Haman's lack of virtue is just a natural outcome of a power- driven life.

Symbolically, Haman's way of life reveals the current condition of virtue—i.e., it can never be naturally maintained. We could claim, like the Enlightenment thinkers, that we are naturally good and have the capacity to overcome all our faults. An ambitious German philosopher, Friedrich Nietzsche, even went so far as to declare that we humans can strive and transcend the limits of this world to the point of becoming a "superhuman" (übermesch). I do not know what Nietzsche meant by a "superhuman," but my guess is that it points to an individual who can overcome his limitations and declare like Napoleon, "The word impossible is not in my dictionary."

Is Haman a representation of this superhuman? Having reached the pinnacle of success, was Haman able to overcome all his limitations? The story of Esther tells us that Haman's self-made success and prosperity did not make him a superhuman. On the contrary, he remains a fool being caught in his own snare of pride. Had Haman learned the ways of virtue, he could have lived differently. But is that possible? Can he throw away his royal titles and trophies and turn into a humble virtuous man that does not seek his own benefit but only the prosperity of others? The odds are too slim. It may be easier for a monkey to turn into a man than Haman to humble himself and bow before a peasant Jew named Mordecai. Virtue in this respect is not for everyone.

Such exclusivity does not mean that virtue is inaccessible, being so sacred that it is not to be found in the everyday life and the life of commoners. Rather, all of us can have it, because, like Esther, God kept a spark of virtue that is still glowing in the most unexpected places in this world. It survives as long as we are willing to serve God. As long as we are willing to sacrifice ourselves for the sake of our neighbors and God, we can keep the fire of virtue burning. The potential is there, and God is waiting for the spark to turn into the flash of fire that could light up the world. The harshness of the reality of the world may be stifling virtue, but it takes only a few good men and women to rekindle and revive the lost passion for godly virtue.

The world needs virtue. Without it, it will self- destruct, or at least, many innocent lives will be lost, and the wickedness of Haman will conquer the land that is once called "good" by God. We must put on our best armor and fight against our own vices to gain a new traction in this world, declaring that what is good, just, and beautiful are better options than what is evil, unjust, and despicable.

In today's world, words or concepts such as "commitment," "sacrifice," "justice," or "goodness" are unpopular; in fact, they are avoided. Seldom people commit to any cause, let alone, sacrifice their time, effort, or life for God and their neighbors. The rule of thumb in today's society is, much like Haman's dictum, "every man for himself." There is no time to show mercy, grace, and kindness. If we do that, we reveal our weaknesses, letting our competitors trample all over us.

Moreover, the meaning of what is good, just, and beautiful is indeterminate. As the saying goes, "beauty is in the eye of the beholder." In a pluralistic society where poly-idealism is accepted, my next- door neighbor's concept of justice is as good as what is revealed in the Bible. French Philosopher Jean- Francois Lyotard once quipped that it is a lost cause to try and locate the universal meaning in a world that is complexified like the variegated sand grains in the beach. For him, it is better for us to live with fragmented ideas that highlight each situation and each context in which the idea in question finds its true meaning and value.

Perhaps, existentialists are right to say that man's existence is filled with anxiety. Due to the chaotic nature of the world, we are always afraid of falling into the pit of meaninglessness. We may search for truth, meaning, and value in life, but as we embark on that journey, we will all the more entangle ourselves with the thread of unknowns and indeterminism. The survivalist's trick is, as Lyotard has said, to live with the fragmented world and give up searching for the one truth.

By contrast, Esther tells a different story. She speaks to us with a clear and distinct voice telling us that we should neither shun truth nor live with fragmented ideas in this world. There is a holistic vision of the world that could save us from having to live with anxiety and inauthenticity for the rest of our lives. That holistic vision is none-other than "virtue." Virtue is real and meaningful. It thrives in the world of sacrifice, courage, and wisdom. It is an overarching attitude that could diffuse not only the adverse effects of the power-struggle but also the grotesque behaviors of humankind. It clears up the fogginess of our eyes and helps us recognize our true vocation as well as our life's goal. We are not simply made to be greedy and destructive. Rather, we are made to build up and heal what is hurt, broken, and dying. Our job is to renew the face of the earth so that the glory of God can be restored. We cannot continue to taint and veil His glory and let darkness roam free. The world we live in is too valuable and precious to leave it in the hands of the dark forces.

Sadly, virtue does not guarantee a happy ending like Esther, for there is no proper reward for living a virtuous life in this world. Instead, it may lead to mockery, disrespect, and deprivation. Sacrifice does not guarantee prosperity and riches. Courage may mean imprisonment and torture. Crying out for goodness, justice, and beauty may demand more than just pain and suffering but even death. Jesus' cross proves that point.

The oppression comes because the world is enchanted by the devil's spell of self-centeredness and myopic egotism. The standing rule of the world is, "what's in it for me?" For this reason, the meaning of virtue has been redefined in this context. Virtue is good only if it benefits "me" more than the others.

Moreover, the general public does not want to hear a story that is too idealistic or fairy-tale like. We are living in a world that is scientifically advanced and morally legalistic. The romance of biblical virtue is a thing of the past. Mordecai's donning of the royal robe is far from the reality of this world. There is no more glory of royal virtue in this world.

There is a gap. The world of Esther and the world of today became so far apart that the world of Esther seems to be made up of too-good-to-be-true figures more so than the real-world characters of today. It wasn't supposed to be this way. The two worlds should be correlatable and relatable. What happened in between? We can blame it on time. Surely, thousands of years have passed since Esther's glorious days.

But time is not the main culprit. It is us who have decided to shift our attention away from the temple of God and focus on the tower of Babel. We did not want to smell the purifying scent of incense in God's kingdom but followed our nose and sat with drunkards and power mongrels to gain a favor from the secular authority. We let Haman come back to life, allowing Esther to die. It seems that Queen Esther has taken the same fate as Queen Vashti. The general public has condemned Esther and sided with power mongrels.

If we take our fingers off the pages of Esther and flip through the pages of the Bible, we can easily encounter other narratives that are less "romantic" than Esther. The persecutions and deaths of prophets are good examples. Hebrew 11 lists the horrible endings of our faith heroes. Even Jesus Christ, our Suffering Servant, had to die on the cross, enduring excruciating pain and humiliation. The cross was the wage of his virtue.

Thus, virtue may not guarantee a "good" and "comfortable" life. Rather, it may lead to pain and suffering. However, in spite of it, we are called to be virtuous. We need to make a difference in this world, and without virtue, it is impossible to do so. We must change the course of our "pur" (destiny). We need to pick ourselves up and recover the lost virtue of God's kingdom. Let us not forget to hear the voice of one calling in the virtue-less desert, "Prepare the way for the Lord; make straight in the desert a highway for our God" (Isa 40:3). By doing this, in the end, we will not only receive the crown of glory but also see the true glory of God.

Endnotes

[i] In the NIV, the name of the Persian king is denoted as "Xerxes," but in original Hebrew, it is recorded as "Ahasuerus." For example, see NRSV or NKJ. Since Ahasuerus is commonly understood as Xerxes, we will follow the NIV rendering.

[ii] The Rabbis of the Oral Torah also speculate that Vashti refused the king's order because he demanded her to be naked, wearing only her crown. It explains that Queen Vashti's skin condition made her reject the king's summon. Whether this interpretation is true or not, Queen Vashti's refusal led to her demise.

[iii] Historian Homa Katouzian notes in this regard. "Xerxes was an ill-tempered ruler with proclivities to impulsive and cruel behaviors." For more details, see Heather Neilson, "Herodotus in Fiction: Gore Vidal's Creation" in Brill's Companion to the Reception of Herodotus in Antiquity and Beyond, ed. Jessica Priestley and Vasiliki Zali (Boston: Brill, 2016), 379.

[iv] As an example, see Hugh of St. Victor on the Sacraments of the Christian Faith (Eugene: Wipf and Stock, 2007).

[v] Andre LaCocque notes that, "although the historical Xerxes inaugurated the practice of monogamy in the dynasty, he kept a harem with hundreds of concubines and was known for his numerous adulterous love affairs." For more details, See Andrew LaCocque, Esther Regina: A Bakhtinian Reading (Chicago: Northwestern University, 2007).

www.ingramcontent.com/pod-product-compliance
Lightning Source LLC
Chambersburg PA
CBHW070127030426
42335CB00016B/2291